KT-463-270

first book of aircraft

Isabel Thomas

C015849295

For Harry, Joey and Oscar

Published 2013 by
A&C Black
An imprint of Bloomsbury Publishing Plc
50 Bedford Square, London, WC1B 3DP

www.bloomsbury.com

ISBN 978-1-4081-9293-1

Copyright © 2013 Bloomsbury Publishing Plc
Text copyright © 2013 Isabel Thomas
Illustrations: Barry Croucher

The right of Isabel Thomas to be identified as the author of this work has been asserted by her in accordance with the Copyrights, Designs and Patents Act 1988.

A CIP catalogue for this book is available from the British Library.

All rights reserved. No part of this publication may be reproduced in any form or by any means – graphic, electronic or mechanical, including photocopying, recording, taping or information storage and retrieval systems – without the prior permission in writing of the publishers.

This book is produced using paper that is made from wood grown in managed, sustainable forests. It is natural, renewable and recyclable. The logging and manufacturing processes conform to the environmental regulations of the country of origin.

Printed in China by C&C.

10 9 8 7 6 5 4 3 2 1

Contents

Introduction	5
Hot air balloon	6
Airship	7
Hang glider	8
Paraglider	9
Helicopter	10–11
Gyroplane	12
Light aircraft	13
Microlight	14
Glider	15
Stunt plane	16
Business aircraft	17
Cargo plane	18–19
Twin prop aeroplane	20
Twin jet aeroplane	21
Trijet aeroplane	22
Jumbo jet	23
Superjumbo	24–25
Supersonic jet	26
Vintage aircraft	27

Biplane 28
Triplane 29
Combat aircraft 30
Strike aircraft 31
Tiltrotor 32–33
Unmanned Aircraft System (UAS) 34
Flying wing 35
Vertical take-off and landing jet 36
Flying car 37
Seaplane 38–39
Space plane 40

Useful words 41

Spotter's guide 42-47

Find out more 48

Aircraft safety
Aircraft are powerful machines. They can be very dangerous.
Always have an adult with you when you look at aircraft.
Do not stand close to aircraft.

Aircraft

The sky is full of exciting flying machines. Look out for gliders and hot air balloons. Listen out for the roar of a jet plane and the buzz of helicopters.

You can spot aircraft at airports, air shows, museums, and in the sky. This book will help you to name the aircraft you see. It tells you how they work and shows you what special features to look out for.

At the back of this book is a Spotter's Guide to help you remember the aircraft you find. Tick them off as you spot them. You can also find out the meaning of some useful words here.

Turn the page to find out all about aircraft!

Hot air balloon

Look for colourful hot air balloons on sunny days. They carry passengers over countryside and cities. The pilot can make the balloon go up or down. It travels slowly, in the same direction as the wind.

Balloon made of nylon

The burner heats the air inside the balloon. The hot air rises.

The pilot lands by letting hot air out of the balloon. The balloon sinks back to the ground.

Skirt made of fireproof material

Burner

Wicker basket carries passengers

Fuel tanks

Airship

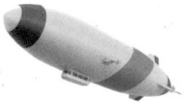

An airship is like a huge helium balloon. It is filled with a gas that is lighter than air. The gas helps the airship to rise up into the air without using much engine power.

This airship carries tourists in California, USA.

Layers of fabric and plastic

Plastic and metal frame inside

Longer than a jumbo jet

Rear engine pushes the airship through the air

Two pilots

Cabin for up to 12 passengers

Side engine steers the airship

Fins help with steering

Hang glider

Hang glider pilots swoop and soar like birds, hanging below a giant wing. Hang gliders do not have engines. They hitch a lift on rising warm air.

The wing is made of fabric wrapped around a metal skeleton.

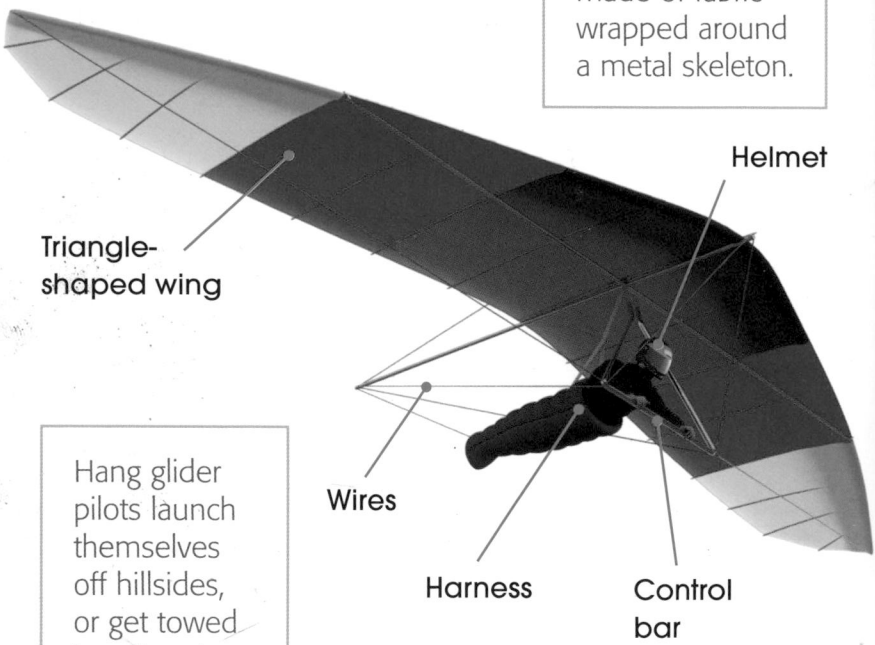

Hang glider pilots launch themselves off hillsides, or get towed into the air.

The pilot steers by moving her body from side to side.

Paraglider

This parachute does not drop from a plane. It takes off from the ground! The pilot sits in a special harness. She steers the paraglider by moving her body, and pulling cables.

Paragliders are the only aircraft that can be packed into a rucksack.

Soft fabric sail

Lines

Most paragliders have no engine. Moving air carries them up into the sky.

Flight suit

Helmet

Controls

Reserve parachute

Harness

Helicopter

Rotors let helicopters fly forwards, backwards, and sideways. They don't need a runway to take off and land. Helicopters can also hover. This lets them pick things up without landing.

Helicopters are very useful in an emergency. This rescue helicopter picks up injured people in the mountains.

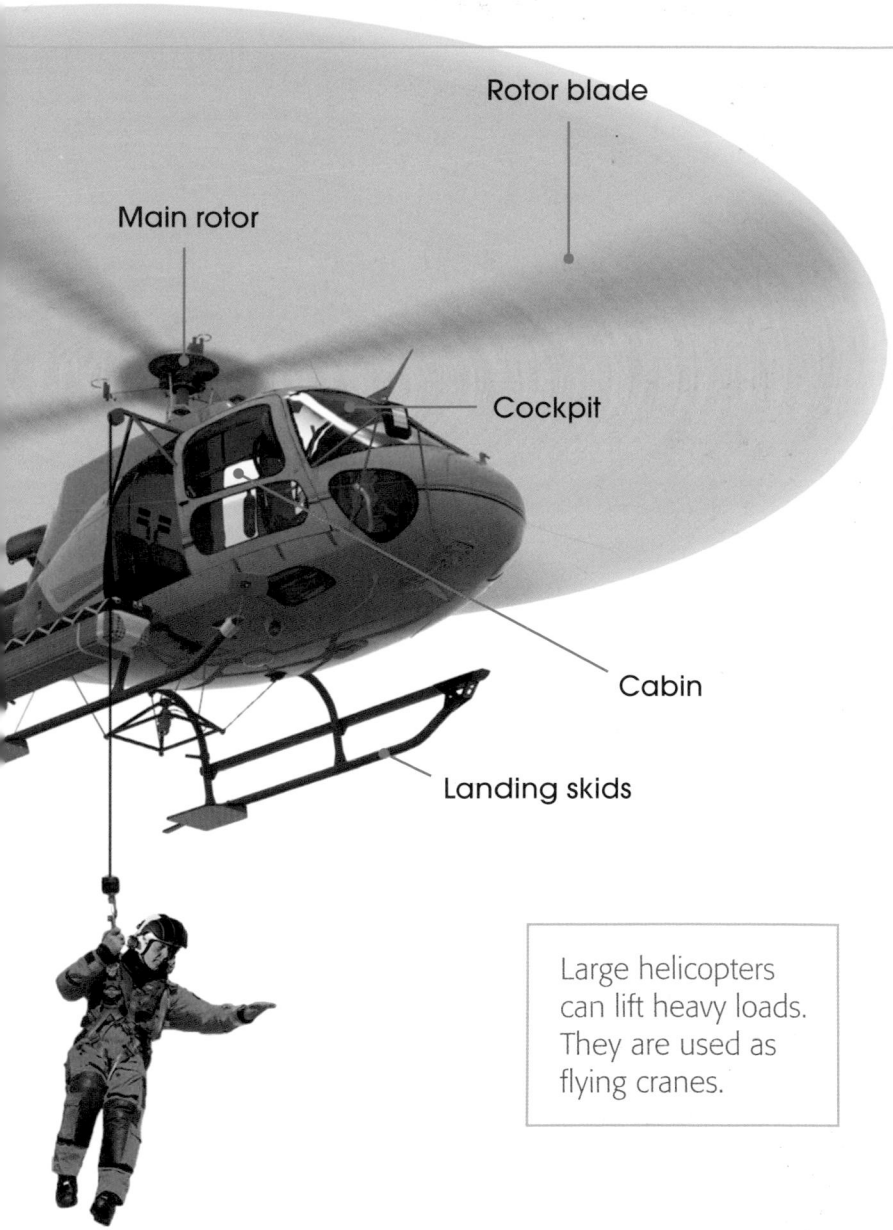

Large helicopters can lift heavy loads. They are used as flying cranes.

Gyroplane

This aircraft looks like a helicopter. But it works in a different way. A propeller engine pushes the gyroplane forwards. The rotor blades are pushed around by air, like a windmill. This lifts the gyroplane into the air.

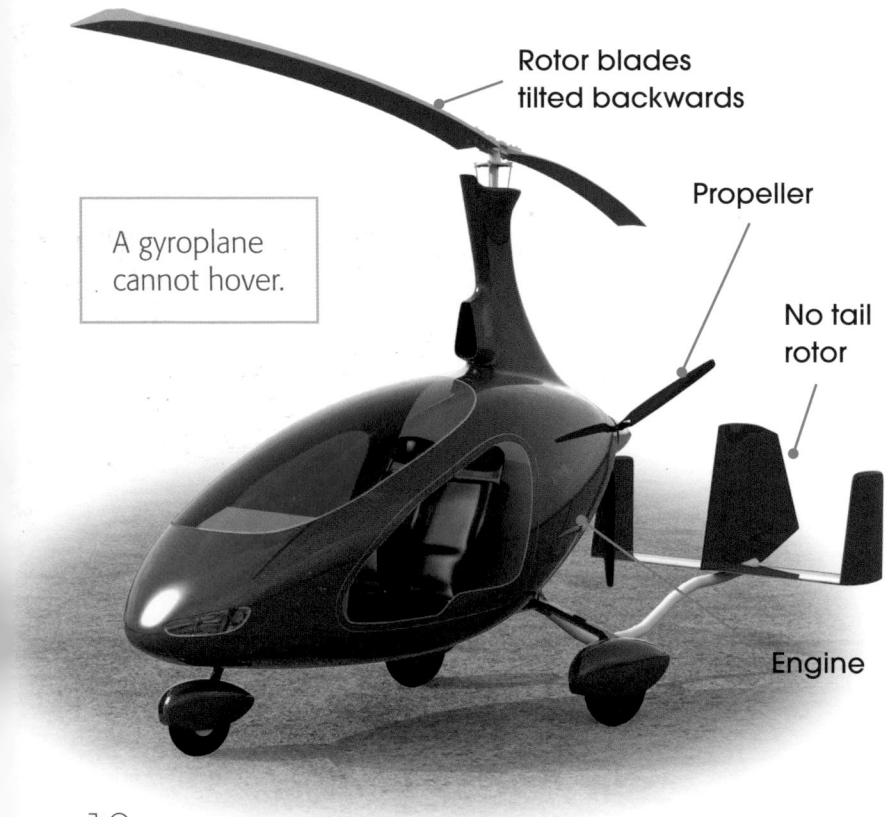

A gyroplane cannot hover.

Light aircraft

Light aircraft are the cars of the sky. People learn to fly them for fun, and for sport. They are also used as small business, passenger, and cargo planes.

This Cessna Caravan carries up to 14 passengers.

Wings high on body

Propeller

Wheels do not fold into fuselage

Piston engine

Microlight

These tiny aircraft are like hang gliders with engines. Wheels let them take off and land on flat ground. You might spot one taking off from a beach.

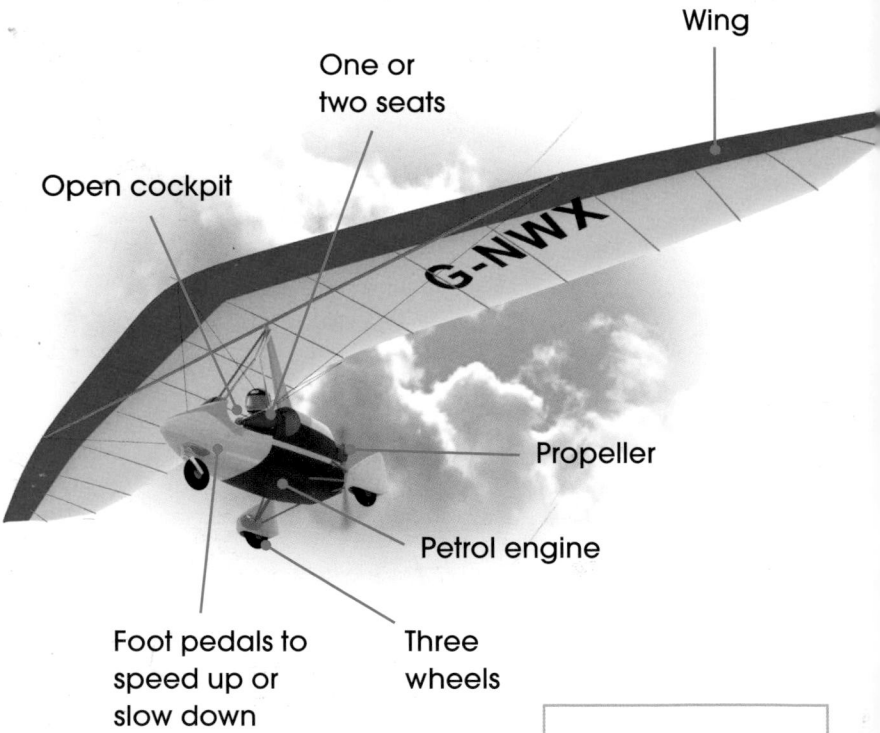

Some microlights come in a box to build at home.

Glider

You might spot gliders in the countryside. Most gliders do not have an engine. They are towed or launched into the air. Once they are up, they can glide and soar for hours.

People fly gliders for fun and for sport.

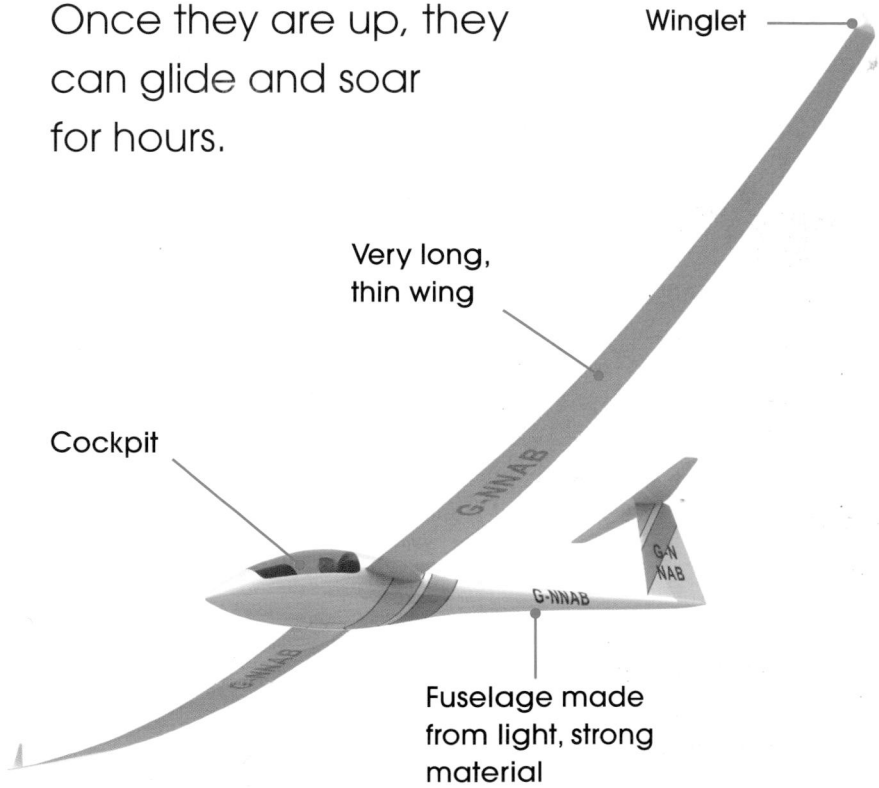

Stunt plane

This plane is specially designed for stunts. It is light but very strong. Look out for planes like this at air shows. They roll, spin, and loop-the-loop to amaze the crowds.

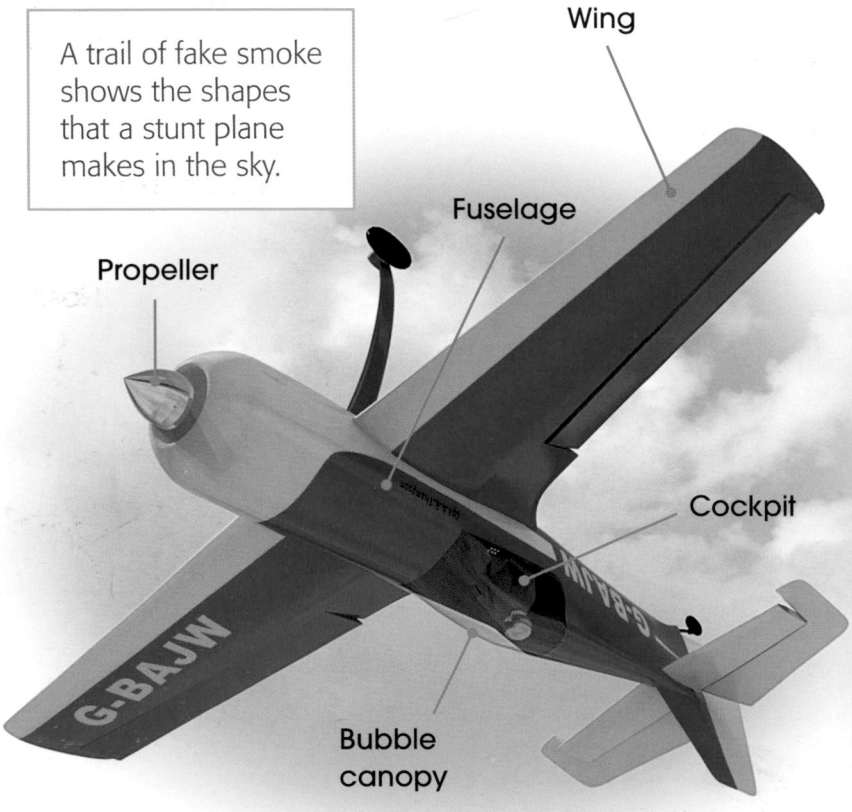

Business aircraft

A private plane is useful for people who fly often for work. It can travel wherever they need to go, whenever they want to leave. The fastest business aircraft have jet engines.

The cabin of this Learjet is a comfortable place to work. Passengers can even hold meetings in the air.

Small cabin

Jet engines at back of plane

Nose

Wing

Fuselage

Winglets for a smooth, fast ride

Cargo plane

These huge aircraft carry goods from place to place. There is a large door at the back or front. Sometimes the whole nose lifts up to load and unload cargo.

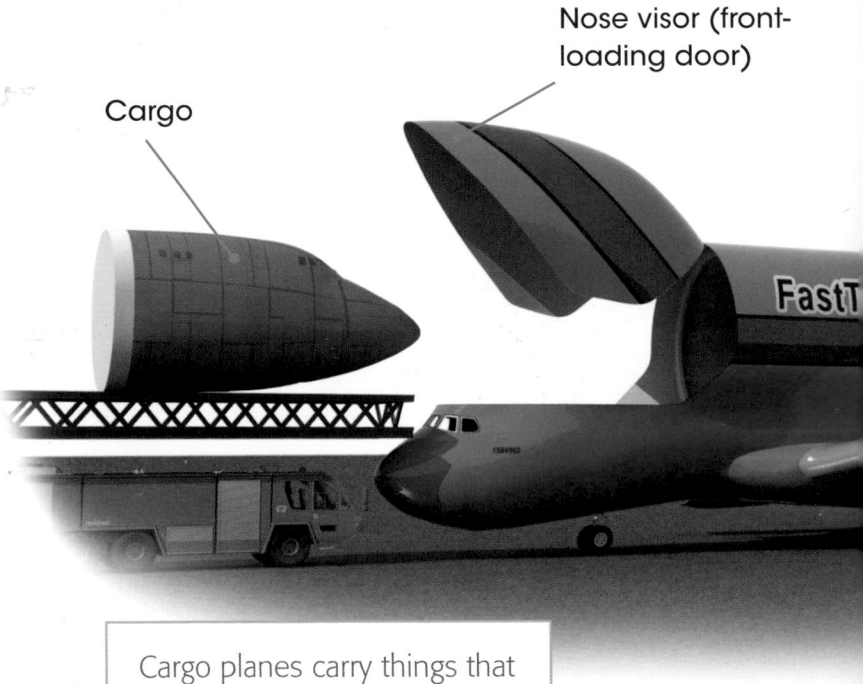

Cargo planes carry things that need to be delivered quickly, such as post and fresh food.

Some cargo planes can drop their load while they are flying. The goods are attached to parachutes and fall slowly to the ground.

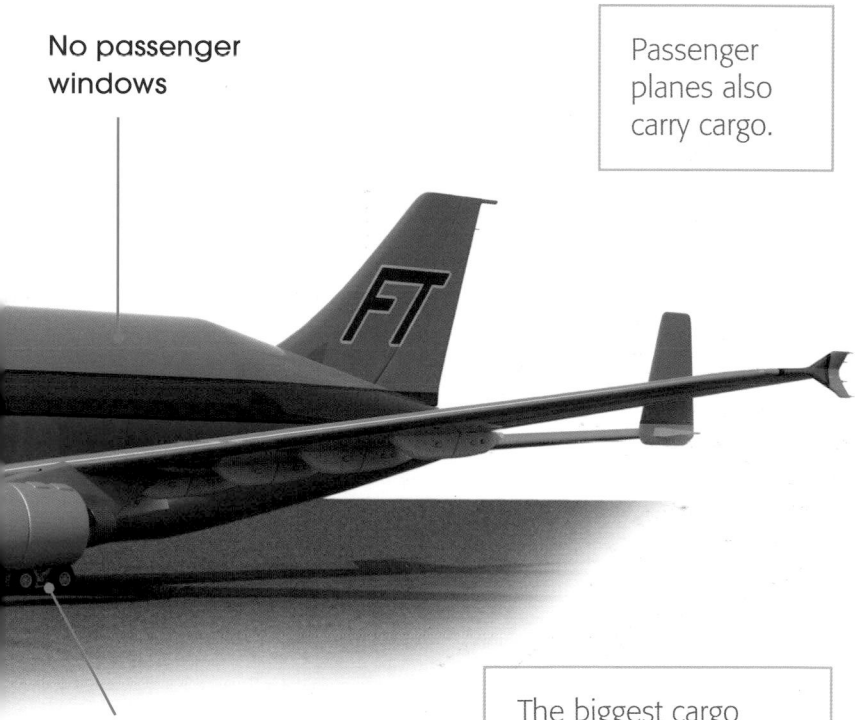

Passenger planes also carry cargo.

The biggest cargo planes have humped bodies. They can carry extra-large cargo, such as other aircraft.

Twin prop aeroplane

This airliner has two turboprop engines. These are jet engines that turn propellers. You can spot them on airliners that make short or medium-sized journeys.

Many cargo planes have turboprop engines.

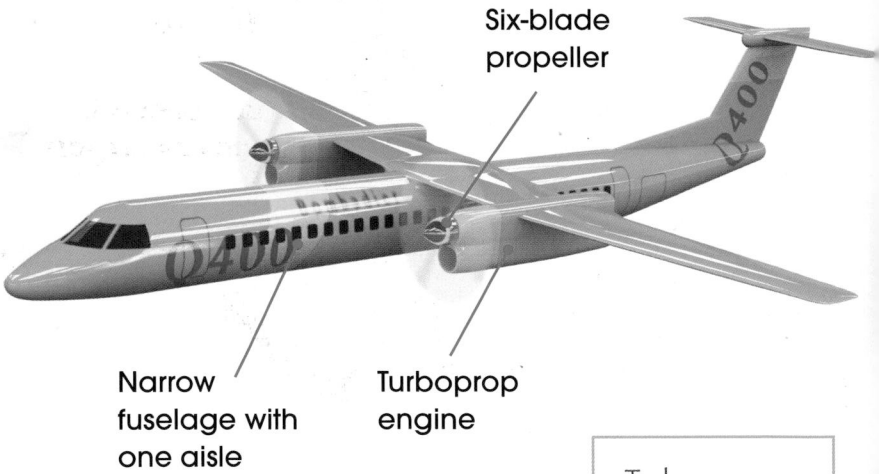

Turboprop engines can be very noisy.

Twin jet aeroplane

Most airliners have turbofan jet engines. These engines are smooth, quiet and fast. Small and medium-sized airliners only need two jet engines.

Boeing 737s carry millions of people on holiday every year.

Tail decorated with airline logo

Main deck for passengers and crew

6 passengers in each row of seats

Birdproof windshield

Cargo deck for luggage and cargo

Trijet aeroplane

Aeroplanes powered by three jet engines are tricky to spot. Very few are made each year. Their extra engine makes them very safe to fly. If one engine breaks down, the plane still has two engines to land with.

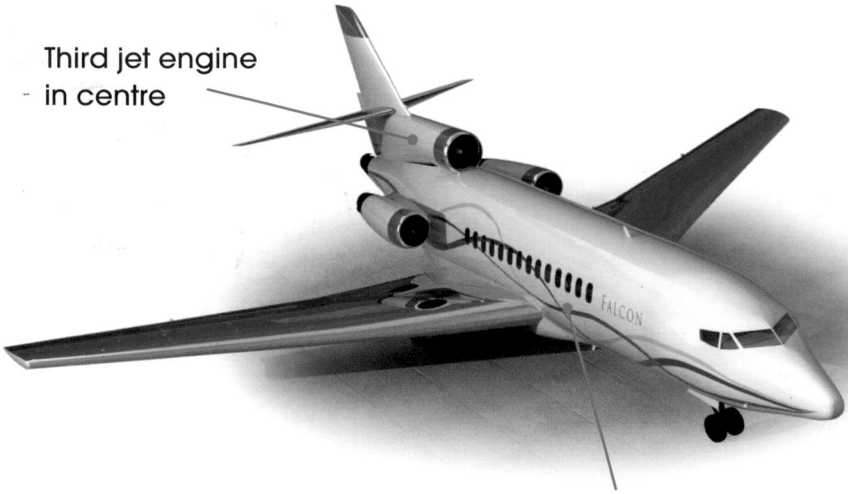

This Dassault Falcon is being used as a business jet.

Jumbo jet

The biggest jet airliners are known as jumbo jets. They usually fly long distances. They can fit up to ten passengers in every row.

Forty-five cars could fit on the wing of this Boeing 747.

Upper deck inside hump

Passenger cabin with room for 345 passengers

Fin

Tail

Flight deck

Four jet engines

Wide body with two aisles

Superjumbo

If you visit an airport, look out for an Airbus A380.

The A380 is so big, there are lifts between its decks.

It is the world's biggest airliner. More than 800 passengers can fly at once.

First class passengers can book private rooms with full-sized beds.

Supersonic jet

Supersonic aircraft can fly faster than sound travels. Look out for supersonic military planes. If one flies past, you will hear a loud boom, like thunder.

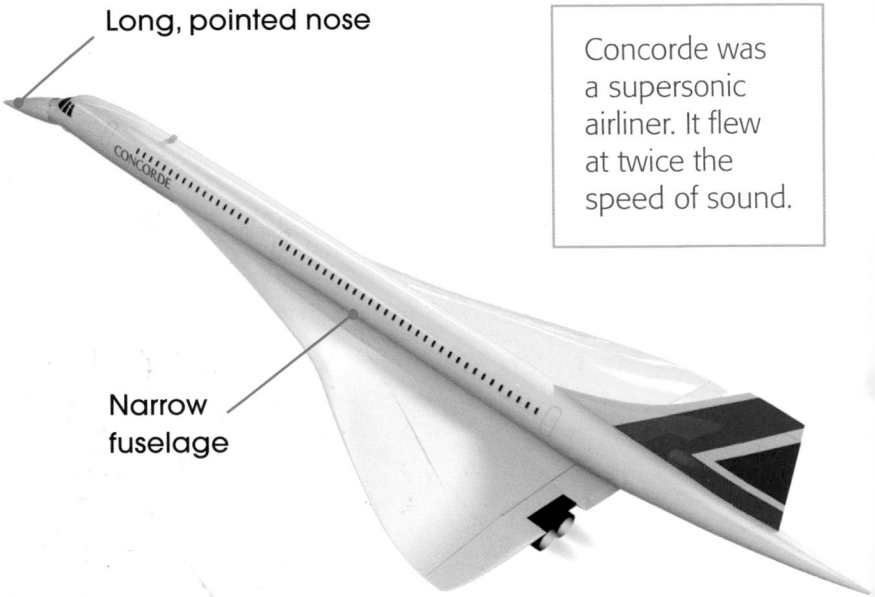

Concorde was a supersonic airliner. It flew at twice the speed of sound.

Concorde stopped flying in 2003, but you can still see them in aircraft museums.

Vintage aircraft

At aircraft museums, you can climb onboard aircraft from the past. But it's even better to see one fly! Many old aircraft have been kept working. You can see them in action at air shows.

Propeller

Four machine guns in each wing

Piston engine

Single seat

Camouflage pattern

Armour plating

This Spitfire was a fighter plane in World War Two.

Biplane

Biplanes have two wings on each side. The wings are joined together by struts.

The world's first proper aeroplane was a biplane, called the Wright Flyer.

The extra wings let this biplane fly very slowly. This is useful for spraying crops, or putting out forest fires.

Triplane

Some of the very first aeroplanes had three wings on each side. They are called triplanes. This one was a fighter plane in World War One.

Triplanes are slower than other types of planes. They are very rare today.

Strut

Open cockpit

Wooden propeller

Combat aircraft

This fighter jet is one of the most amazing aircraft in the world. It can fly faster than the speed of sound. Powerful computers help it to find and attack enemy targets in the sky.

Ejection seats blast fighter pilots out of their plane in an emergency.

Strike aircraft

Bombers attack enemy targets on the ground. They are specially designed to carry heavy loads.

Tail fin

Wings swing back for high speed flight

Seat for a weapons operator

Pilot

Weapons carried under fuselage and wings

When this Tornado takes off, its wings stick straight out to the side. This helps lift the plane into the sky. The wings swing back for flying at high speed.

Tiltrotor

What do you get if you cross an aeroplane with a helicopter? A tiltrotor! This amazing aircraft can tilt its engines as it flies.

It takes off, lands and hovers like a helicopter.

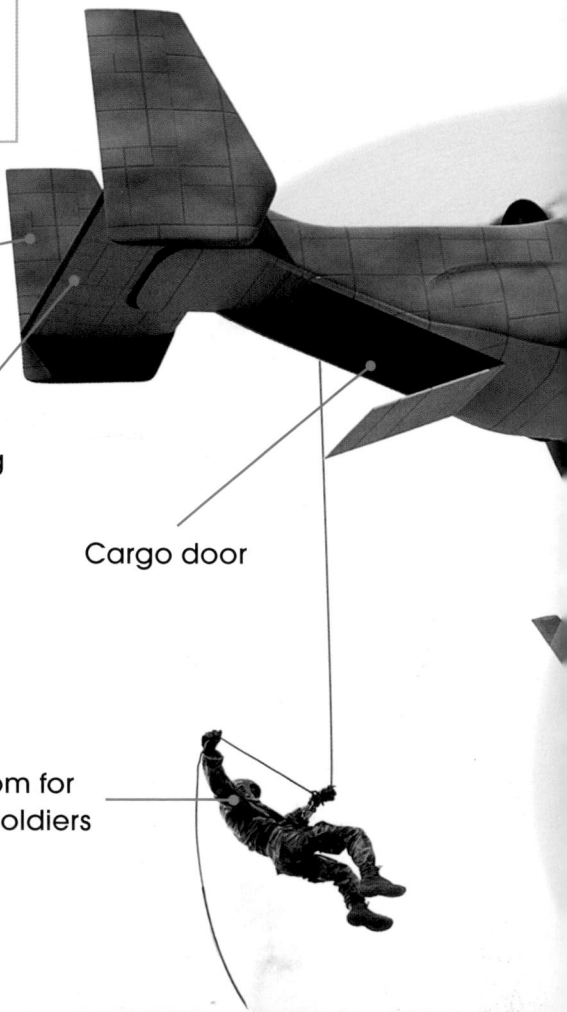

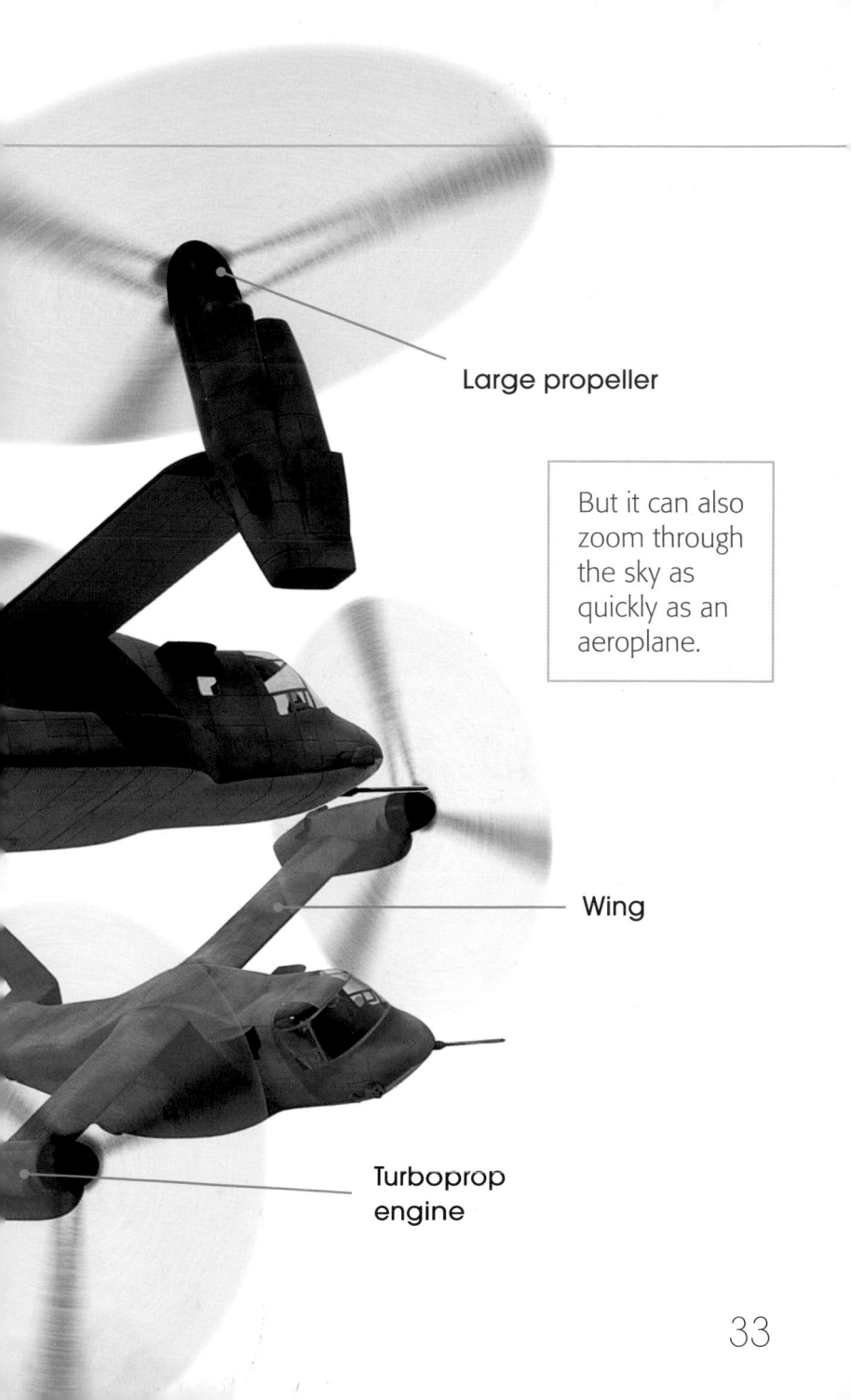

But it can also zoom through the sky as quickly as an aeroplane.

Unmanned Aircraft System (UAS)

What is missing from this aeroplane? The pilot! A powerful computer flies the plane.

Unmanned military aircraft can fly into dangerous areas. No pilot is in danger if they are attacked.

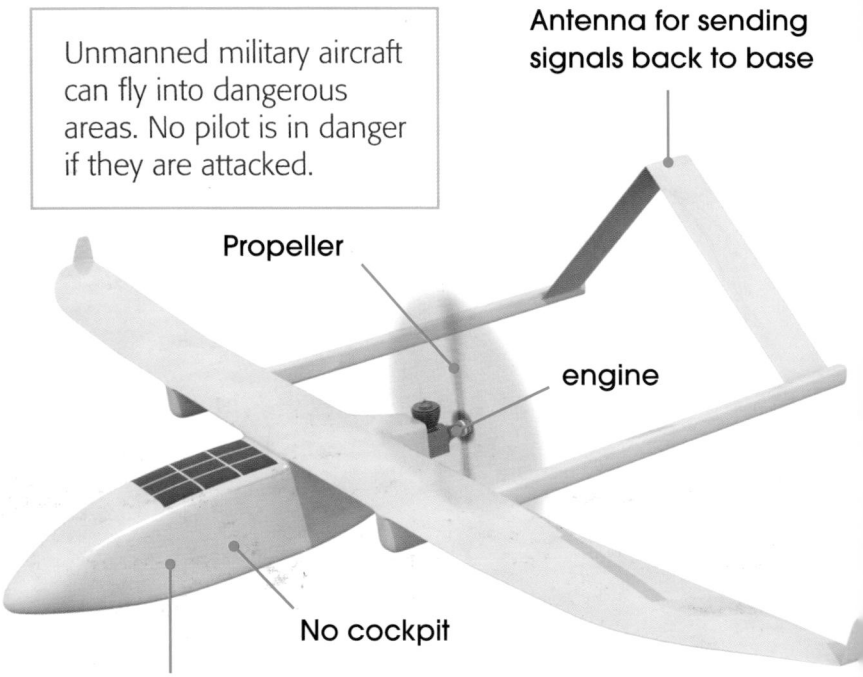

Unmanned aircraft have been flown into hurricanes and cyclones. They send information back to scientists on the ground.

Flying wing

Flying wings have no fuselage or tail. The cockpit, engines, fuel tanks and cargo are all inside one large, triangle-shaped wing.

Flying wings travel very smoothly through the air. This helps military aircraft to hide from enemies.

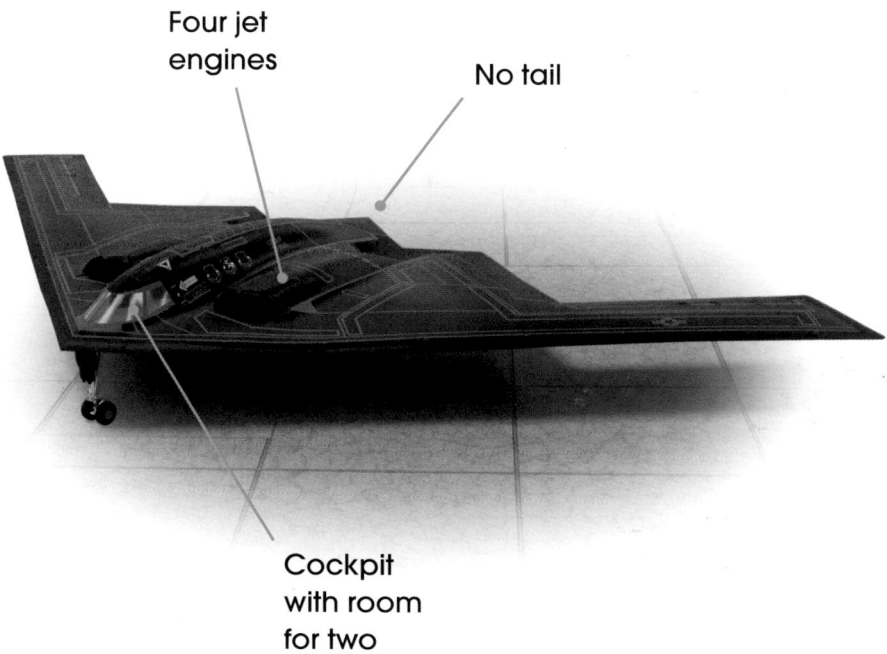

Vertical take-off and landing jet

This is a special plane. Its jet engine has a nozzle that can be pointed downwards. This lets it hover in the air, and land without a runway.

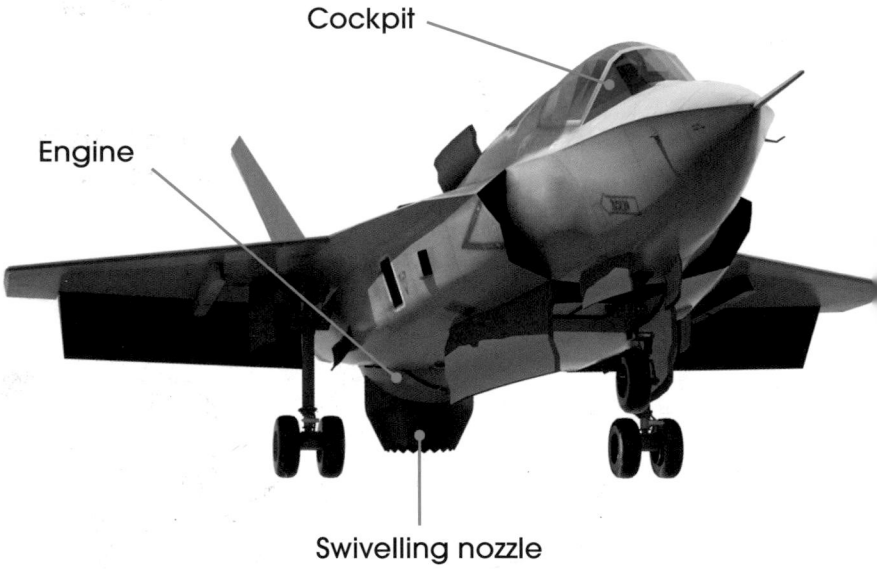

This fighter jet can easily land on an aircraft carrier at sea.

Flying car

Folding the wings of this aeroplane turns it into a road vehicle. It can be kept in a normal garage. The pilot can drive it to the airport!

Propeller

Cockpit with room for pilot and a passenger

Folding wing

Wing folds in two places

Wingmirrors tuck in for flying

Headlights for driving on the road

Cargo area

Four wheels

Space plane

A powerful rocket engine blasts this aircraft into space. It uses its wings to glide back down to Earth afterwards.

Wings don't work in space because there is no air. A space plane flies like a spaceship in space, using thrusters to steer.

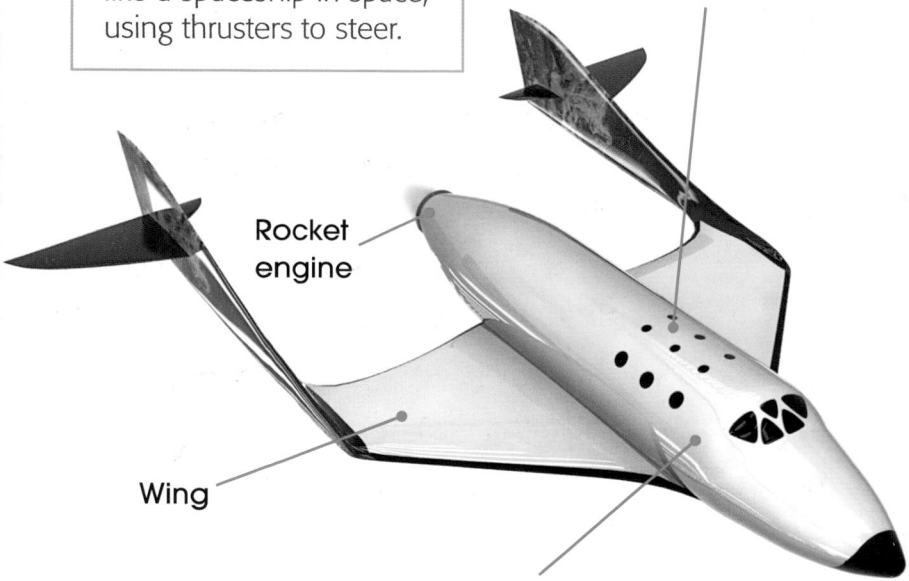

Useful words

cabin the place where passengers sit

cockpit where the pilot sits

flight deck where the pilot and crew sit on a large aircraft

fuselage the body of an aeroplane

jet engine an engine that burns fuel to produce a jet of hot gas and move an aircraft forwards

landing gear the wheels that an aircraft rests on when it's not flying

piston engine an engine that burns fuel to move pistons up and down, which turns a propeller

propeller blades that spin around vertically, pushing an aircraft forwards

rotor blades that spin around horizontally, lifting an aircraft into the air

wing the part that supports the rest of the aircraft in the air

winglet the turned-up end of some aeroplane wings, to help the plane to travel more smoothly through the air

Spotter's guide

How many of these aircraft have you seen? Tick them when you spot them.

☐ Hot air balloon
page 6

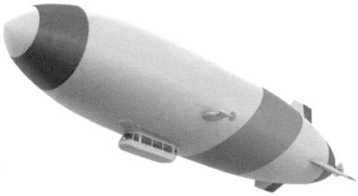

☐ Airship
page 7

☐ Hang glider
page 8

☐ Paraglider
page 9

Helicopter
page 10

Gyroplane
page 12

Light aircraft
page 13

Microlight
page 14

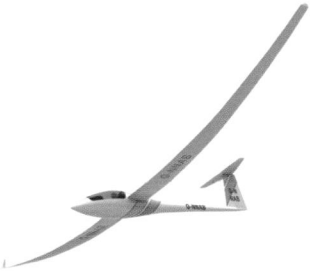

Glider
page 15

Stunt plane
page 16

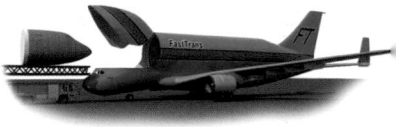

Business aircraft
page 17

Cargo plane
page 18

Twin prop
aeroplane
page 20

Twin jet
aeroplane
page 21

Trijet aeroplane
page 22

Jumbo jet
page 23

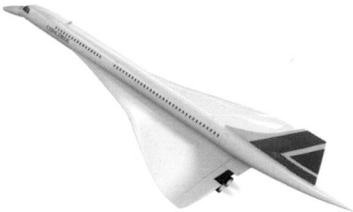

Superjumbo
page 24

Supersonic jet
page 26

Vintage aircraft
page 27

Biplane
page 28

Triplane
page 29

Combat aircraft
page 30

Strike aircraft
page 31

Tiltrotor
page 32

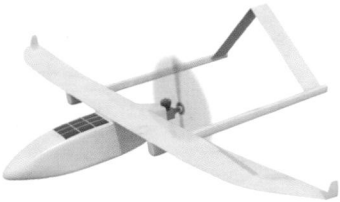

Unmanned Aircraft System (UAS)
page 34

Flying wing
page 35

Vertical take-off and landing jet
page 36

Flying car
page 37

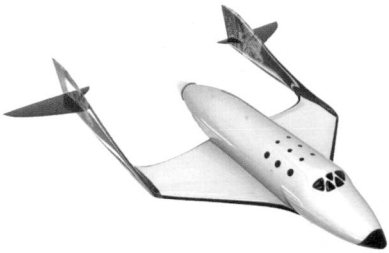

Seaplane
page 38

Space plane
page 40

Find out more

If you would like to find out more about aircraft, you could visit an aircraft museum or air show. You can also look at these websites.

Imperial War Museum Duxford
www.iwm.org.uk/visits/iwm-duxford

Yorkshire Air Museum
www.yorkshireairmuseum.org/

Royal Airforce Museum London and Cosford
www.rafmuseum.org.uk

Royal International Air Tattoo
www.airtattoo.com/

Farnborough International Airshow
www.farnborough.com/

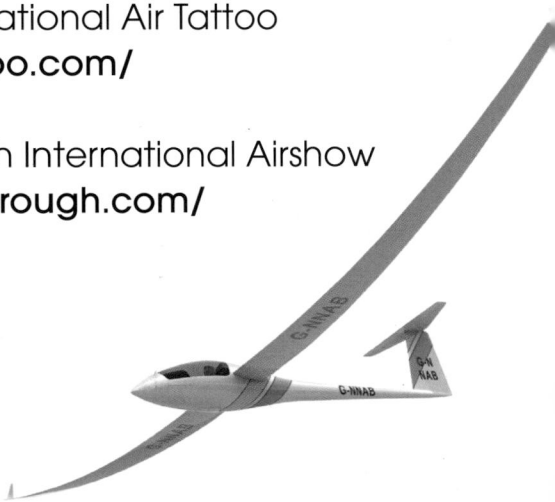